THE

1994-2021

Quiz Book

By

Andrew Shaw

1994-2021

1994-2021

Darts fan by the grace of god

Copyright © 2021 Andrew Shaw

All rights reserved.

ISBN: 9798541004557

This book is available to download for Amazon Kindle or buy a paperback at www.amazon.co.uk

DEDICATION

This book is dedicated to my father,
John Thomas Shaw.
28/10/1939 - 24/05/2018
An avid sports fan and a keen darts fan.
Sadly, taken away too early, aged 78.
R.I.P. Pops

&

Elizabeth Wilson "Betty"
27/08/1938-14/06/2019
Without you, none of this would have been possible.
R.I.P. Betty

CONTENTS

ii Acknowledgement's

1	1994	Pages 1-2
2	1995	Pages 5-6
3	1996	Pages 9-10
4	1997	Pages 13-14
5	1998	Pages 17-18
6	1999	Pages 21-22
7	2000	Pages 25-26
8	2001	Pages 29-30
9	2002	Pages 33-34
10	2003	Pages 37-38
11	2004	Pages 41-42
12	2005	Pages 45-46
13	2006	Pages 49-50
14	2007	Pages 53-54
15	2008	Pages 57-58
16	2009	Pages 61-62
17	2010	Pages 65-66
18	2011	Pages 69-70
19	2012	Pages 73-74
20	2013	Pages 77-78
21	2014	Pages 81-82
22	2015	Pages 85-86
23	2016	Pages 89-90
24	2017	Pages 93-94
25	2018	Pages 97-98
26	2019	Pages 101-102
27	2020	Pages 105-106
28	2021	Pages 109-110

Answers

1 Answers	1994	Page 109
2 Answers	1995	Page 110
3 Answers	1996	Page 111
4 Answers	1997	Page 112
5 Answers	1998	Page 113
6 Answers	1999	Page 114
7 Answers	2000	Page 115
8 Answers	2001	Page 116
9 Answers	2002	Page 117
10 Answers	2003	Page 118
11 Answers	2004	Page 119
12 Answers	2005	Page 120
13 Answers	2006	Page 121
14 Answers	2007	Page 122
15 Answers	2008	Page 123
16 Answers	2009	Page 124
17 Answers	2010	Page 125
18 Answers	2011	Page 126
19 Answers	2012	Page 127
20 Answers	2013	Page 128
21 Answers	2014	Page 129
22 Answers	2015	Page 130
23 Answers	2016	Page 131
24 Answers	2017	Page 132
25 Answers	2018	Page 133
26 Answers	2019	Page 134
27 Answers	2020	Page 135
28 Answers	2021	Page 136

ACKNOWLEDGMENTS

With many thanks to the Professional Darts Corporation
And players, families, friends, and supporters of darts.
Who without them, this book would not be possible.

1. 1994

Question 1.

Who won the first ever WDC World Championship?

Question 2

And who was runner up in the first ever World Championship final?

Question 3

Where was the first World Championship final held?

Question 4

Who won the first World Matchplay??

Question 5

Where was the first world Matchplay held?

1994-2021

Question 6

How much did the first World champion win?

Question 7

Who is "The Artist" winner of the bronze bully on Bullseye this year?

Question 8

Which new TV company, signed a deal to cover the World Championships and World Matchplay?

Question 9

Who sponsored the first World championship finals?

Question 10

World Matchplay quarter finalist, later a caller known as "The Voice"?

1994-2021

2. 1995

Question 11

Who was the 1995 World Champion?

Question 12

And who did he beat in the World Championship final?

Question 13

Known as "Stoneface" which former BDO World champion, was a PDC World championship semifinalist this year?

Question 14

Which duo won the first ever PDC World pairs?

Question 15

Which Scotsman made his last ever TV appearance in the world Matchplay this year??

1994-2021

Question 16

World Matchplay runner up, known as "Big Cliff"?

Question 17

Which car company sponsored the World championships?

Question 18

World Matchplay quarter finalist, born in Liss, England?

Question 19

Chesterfield dart player finished 3rd in the world Matchplay?

Question 20

Which player was nicknamed "The Power" from this year?

1994-2021

1994-2021

3. 1996

Question 21

Who won the WDC World Matchplay?

Question 22

Which company sponsored the World Championship finals?

Question 23

Which company sponsored the World Matchplay?

Question 24

And which player nicknamed "Braveheart" was a World championship losing semifinalist?

Question 25

The "Rhinestone cowboy" finished 3rd in the world Matchplay?

Question 26

World pairs winners from England?

Question 27

American "Kevin" hit a 170 finish in the world championship finals?

Question 28

Canadian "The Mauler" played in his first World Championship?

Question 29

"The menace" hit a 101.56 average as runner up in the World Championships?

Question 30

"Wozza" hit a 89.99 average in his quarter final defeat in the World Championship?

1994-2021

4. 1997

Question 31

The WDC became what, in this year?

Question 32

"The Crafty Cockney" WDC World Championship Semi-finalist?

Question 33

WDC/PDC Founder member, who played in the 1994,95,96,97 World Championships.
Whose son is now a PDC Official?

Question 34

Stoke born World Matchplay winner?

Question 35

Lancaster, England born player was World Matchplay runner-up?

Question 36

World Championship finals sponsor?

Question 37

Dutch duo, won the World Pairs?

Question 38

World Championship runner up with a 94.50 average?

Question 39

Peter, World Championship losing semi-finalist?

Question 40

"Dennis, losing World championship finalist with a 96.79 average?

1994-2021

5. 1998

Question 41

"Sharp dressed man" who won the World Matchplay??

Question 42

First wore an Hawaiian shirt for a bet?

Question 43

Who won the WDC World Championship?

Question 44

Venue for the first World Grand Prix?

Question 45

Born in Mexborough, Yorkshire, lost 6-0 in the world championship final?

Question 46

"The Prince of Style" won the World Matchplay?

Question 47

"The Rocket" World Matchplay runner-up?

Question 48

Future commentator, lost in the world Matchplay semi-final?

Question 49

World Championship sponsor?

Question 50

Former BDO World champion, lost in the PDC equivalent semi-final?

1994-2021

6. 1999

Question 51

Who won the WDC World Matchplay?

Question 52

World Championship and World Matchplay runner-up?

Question 53

Was runner up in the BDO World championship before he joined the PDC?

Question 54

Which Singapore born player represented the USA?

Question 55

Born in Winchester, England, lost in the world championship Quarter final?

Question 56

Equalled Snookers Steve Davis, with 5 World Championship titles?

Question 57

Player who walks on to "Cold as Ice" lost in the world Championship quarter final with a 95.00 average?

Question 58

"The Bulldog" lost in the World Championship semi-final with a 94.19 average?

Question 59

"Big Cliff" lost in the World Championship quarter final?

Question 60

What major change happened to the world Championship finals?

1994-2021

7. 2000

Question 61

Which new venue did the World Grand Prix move to?

Question 62

Who was the first World Champion of the new millennium?

Question 63

World Matchplay sponsor?

Question 64

5-time World Champion, played his last game against the USA's Steve Brown?

Question 65

Born in Derby, England hit the only 170 Check-out in this year's Worlds Championship finals?

Question 66

"Smiffy" lost in the World Championship semi-final?

Question 67

"One Dart" lost in the World Championship semi-final with a 99.07 average?

Question 68

Lancashire man was world Matchplay runner-up?

Question 69

Canadian beat Phil Taylor in the World Matchplay quarter final?

Question 70

Returned as World Championship sponsor?

1994-2021

8. 2001

Question 71

"The Iceman" was World Grand Prix winner?

Question 72

Became the first woman to play in a PDC event??

Question 73

Former BDO World Champion, lost in the World Grand Prix semi-final?

Question 74

Welshman, World Matchplay runner-up?

Question 75

Ponytailed player lost in the World Grand Prix semi-final?

Question 76

"The Adonis" was World Matchplay semi-finalist?

Question 77

Where did the World Grand Prix move to?

Question 78

Dutchman was World Grand Prix runner-up?

Question 79

Hit a TV record 106.45 average?

Question 80

Ipswich Town supporter was World Grand Prix runner-up?

9. 2002

Question 81

First PDC televised 9 darter in the World Matchplay?

Question 82

"Wozza" was World Championship Number 1 seed?

Question 83

Bronzed Adonis made his PDC World Championship debut?

Question 84

"Jaws" lost in the world championship semifinal?

Question 85

"The Artist" beat Phil Taylor in the World Grand Prix?

Question 86

"Stoneface" World Matchplay semi-finalist?

Question 87

"Rocky" World Grand Prix runner-up?

Question 88

Lost to Phil Taylor in both the 2001 and 2002 World Championship semi-finals?

Question 89

Canadian hit the highest check-out of 167 in the World Championship finals?

Question 90

"One dart" lost 7-0 in the world championship final?

1994-2021

10. 2003

Question 91

World Championship winner?

Question 92

World Matchplay runner up nicknamed "Hawaii 501"??

Question 93

Londoner Won the Las Vegas desert classic?

Question 94

"The Power" won the first ever UK Open?

Question 95

Runner-up in the first ever UK Open?

Question 96

Where was the first UK Open held?

Question 97

Who sponsored the first UK Open?

Question 98

"The Rhino" lost in the UK Open quarter final?

Question 99

How much did the World Champion win in prize money this year?

Question 100

Dutchman hit the only 170 check-out in the world Championships?

1. 2004

Question 101.

What happened for the first time in the World Championship final this year?

Question 102

Which future pundit was a World Championship semifinalist?

Question 103

Ipswich Town fan was World Championship runner up?

Question 104

Which Dutchman was UK Open winner?

Question 105

Which bookmaker was World Championship sponsor?

Question 106

Which two players hit 170 finishes in the World Championship finals?

Question 107

Bristol born player was World Matchplay runner up?

Question 108

Lancastrian was World Grand Prix runner up?

Question 109

"Jaws" had a 98.62 average in the World Championship 3rd round?

Question 110

Canadian lost in the 3rd round of the World Championships with a 90.09 average?

1994-2021

1994-2021

2. 2005

Question 111

"Special Brew" was UK Open Runner Up?

Question 112

Which new PDC tournament started in the year?

Question 113

Hit the only 170 finish in the World Championships?

Question 114

"Flash" was World Championship runner up?

Question 115

Which 3 time World Champion played in his last World Championship?

Question 116
And who was World Championship Number 1 seed"?

Question 117
Who became the first Master of Darts Champion?

Question 118
Which player gained the nickname "Jackpot" while playing in the Desert Classic in Las Vegas?

Question 119
Who won the world Matchplay with a 170 finish?

Question 120
Which two players were the first inductees in the PDC Hall of Fame?

1994-2021

3. 2006

Question 121

Which Dutchman won the UK Open?

Question 122

"the Power" won the World Matchplay with a 100.8 average?

Question 123

Which Dutchman was the Premier League runner up??

Question 124

"Barney" hit a 9 darter in the Premier League in Bournemouth?

Question 125

Who was the first referee to enter the Hall of Fame?

Question 126

Which Welshman was UK Open runner up?

Question 127

Wolves fan was a World Championship semifinalist?

Question 128

"One Dart" was the World Championship runner up?

Question 129

"The Saint" was a UK Open semifinalist?

Question 130

Canadian who won the Desert Classic?

1994-2021

4. 2007

Question 131

Became the youngest PDC title winner, when lifting the World Matchplay?

Question 132

This was the last World Championships at which venue?

Question 133

"The Hammers" first PDC event was the Grand Slam?

Question 134

"The Machine" won the World Matchplay?

Question 135

Runner up in the World Matchplay, World Grand Prix and the Premier League?

Question 136

Became the youngest PDC World Championship participant aged 16?

Question 137

UK Open runner up?

Question 138

Dutchman made his World Matchplay debut?

Question 139

Which two players with the same surname, played in the World Championships?

Question 140

World Championship winner, after winning the 2006 BDO equivalent?

1994-2021

5. 2008

Question 141

"Chaos" was World Championship runner up?

Question 142

This year was the first World Championship at which venue?

Question 143

"Jaws" was the World Series of Darts runner up?

Question 144

Canadian won the World Championship?

Question 145

Once had the walk on music "Bonkers" won the UK

Open?

Question 146

"Hawaii 501" lost his 4th World Championship semifinal?

Question 147

Which player won the best newcomer award this year?

Question 148

Later to be chairman of the PDPA, lost in the European championship semifinal?

Question 149

Who was voted Players Player of the Year?

Question 150

Which two commentators entered the Hall of Fame?

1994-2021

6. 2009

Question 151

"Ozzy" won the Championship League?

Question 152

"Cobra" hit a 9 darter in the Champions League of Darts?

Question 153

"The Adonis" was the European Championship runner up?

Question 154

"The Power" was voted Players Player of the Year?

Question 155

Which player from Ipswich was the Premier League runner up?

Question 156

Hit the only 170 finish in the World Championships this year?

Question 157

And who was voted Young Player of the Year?

Question 158

Which 2 x World Champion entered the Hall of Fame?

Question 159

Middlesbrough fan was UK Open runner up?

Question 160

Scotsman won the best newcomer award?

1994-2021

7. 2010

Question 161

"The King" was the Players Championship runner up?

Question 162

"Webby" finished 3rd in the World Championship?

Question 163

The first and only to this date,
PDC Women's World Champion?

Question 164

Who won the Young Player of the Year award?

Question 165

Dutchman hit a Premier League 9 darter versus
Terry Jenkins in Aberdeen?

Question 166

Which two directors entered the Hall of Fame?

Question 167

Husband to be of Sammi Marsh, won the Championship League?

Question 168

Dutch pair who won the first World Cup of Darts?

Question 169

Australian who was voted best newcomer?

Question 170

Hit a 9 darter in the Premier League final?

1994-2021

2011

Question 171

Most successful player in history, inducted into the Hall of Fame?

Question 172

Stoke born player, won his first World Championship?

Question 173

"Flying Scotsman" won the Premier League?

Question 174

"Mile High" was voted best newcomer?

Question 175

Hampshire player won the UK Open?

Question 176

Son of Colin, was voted Young Player of the Year?

Question 177

Players Championship runner up "Webby"?

Question 178

Reached his one and only World Championship semifinal?

Question 179

Welshman reached the World Grand Prix semi final

Question 180 (One hundred and eiiigghhttyy ha)

"The Warrior" was UK Open runner up?

9. 2012

Question 181

Player, who lost one eye when he was young, reached the Champions League of Darts Semifinal?

Question 182

Stoke born "Hammer" was World Championship runner up?

Question 183

"The Hurricane" was Players Championship runner up?

Question 184

Won his first PDC title in the World Grand Prix and was voted Young Player of the Year?

Question 185

"Diamond" hit a 9 darter in the Players Championship qualifier in Barnsley?

Question 186

"The King" was World Grand Prix runner up?

Question 187

"Chizzy" won the best newcomer award?

Question 188

Pro tour Player of the Year was which Scotsman?

Question 189

Australian won his first European championship?

Question 190

Scotsman won the UK Open?

1994-2021

10. 2013

Question 191

"Jabba" had back to back Pro Tour wins?

Question 192

1st world Series of Darts was in which city?

Question 193

"The Force" was a World Grand Prix runner up?

Question 194

Which bookmaker, became the new World Matchplay sponsor?

Question 195

Yorkshireman was voted best newcomer?

Question 196

"jackpot" won the European Championship?

Question 197

Won his 1st Premier League, beating Phil Taylor in the final?

Question 198

Another referee entered into the Hall of Fame?

Question 199

Stoke legend won the Grand Slam?

Question 200

And which Scotsman was runner up in the Grand Slam?

1994-2021

1994-2021

2014

Question 201.

Which two players hit nine darts at the World Championship?

Question 202

Which player won his first ever World Championship final?

Question 203

What was unusual about this year's World Championship final?

Question 204

"Jackpot" beat Terry Jenkins in the UK Open final??

Question 205

Caused an upset by beating Phil Taylor 9-7 in the UK Open?

1994-2021

Question 206

The UK Open finals moved to which venue?

Question 207

Hit a nine-dart finish against Michael Smith in the World Macthplay

Question 208

"The Bullet" hit the high 167 finish in the World Matchplay World Matchplay?

Question 209

Which Belgian, hit a nine-dart finish in the Grand Slam?

Question 210

Winner of the World Youth Championship?

1994-2021

1994-2021

2015

Question 211

Which Scotsman was the 2015 World Champion?

Question 212

And which other Scotsman walked 500 miles to win the World Grand Prix?

Question 213

Which player missed out on the Premier League play offs for the first time ever?

Question 214

Which player won his first UK Open?

Question 215

Australian hit the highest finish (167) in the PDC Masters?

Question 216

Hit a nine-dart finish in the World Championship finals?

Question 217

Which player hit a nine-dart finish in the Grand Slam?

Question 218

Which BDO World Champion, finally accepted the PDC invitation to the Grand slam, after declining several times?

Question 219

Which German was World Youth Champion?

Question 220

The "Machine" ended Phil Taylors 38 match unbeaten run at the World Matchplay?

1994-2021

1994-2021

2016

Question 221

Which "Flying" Scotsman hit a nine darter against Jelle Klaasen in the semifinals of the World Championship?

Question 222

"The Power" lost with a 100.3 average in the World Championship last 16?

Question 223

Austrian won the International darts Open?

Question 224

Future World Champion won a Unicorn Challenge Tour event in wigan?

Question 225

"Chuck" hit a nine-dart finish in the Players Championship finals

Question 226

"Kong" was a Players Championship quarter finalist?

Question 227

Canadian hit a maximum 170 checkout along with MVG?

Question 228

Australian World Youth Champion?

Question 229

Which Welsh pair were World Cup of darts runners up?

Question 230

The "Machine" Grand Slam runner up?

1994-2021

1994-2021

2017

Question 231

Which Dutchman was the 2017 World Champion?

Question 232

"Snakebite" won the UK Open?

Question 233

Which Belgian was World Youth Champion?

Question 234

Which Welshman was Players Championship runner up?

Question 235

" Bully Boy" was World Series of Darts runner up?

Question 236

Which Dutch pair was World Cup of Darts winners?

Question 237

"The Power" won the World Matchplay?

Question 238

Which Austrian won the Champions League of Darts?

Question 239

"Iceman" was UK Open runner up?

Question 240

Which Northern Irishman won the World Grand Prix?

1994-2021

1994-2021

2018

Question 241

Which Belgian hit a nine-dart finish in the Grand Slam of Darts?

Question 242

Which Englishman won his first World Championship title?

Question 243

Which Welshman won the Grand Slam of Darts?

Question 244

Which Northern Irishman won the Players Championship

Question 245

Which Republic of Ireland pair lost in the final of the World Cup of Darts?

Question 246

Which tournament had NO Englishman in the last eight?

Question 247

"Diamond" won the Dutch darts Championship?

Question 248

Which German, won the German darts Open?

Question 249

"The Machine" won the European Championship?

Question 250

"Flying Scotsman" won the World Matchplay and UK Open?

1994-2021

1994-2021

2019

Question 251

"Bully Boy" 2019 World Championship runner up?

Question 252

"Iceman" won the World Grand Prix?

Question 253

First Austrian to play in the Premier League?

Question 254

"Voltage" won the World Matchplay?

Question 255

"The Asp" won the UK Open?

Question 256

"Cool Hand Luke" beat defending champion Rob Cross 4-2 in the World Championships?

Question 257

MVG Won his 5th Premier League title?

Question 258

"Chizzy" was the World Grand Prix runner up?

Question 259

Which Scottish pair won the World Cup?

Question 260

And which Irish pair were World Cup runners up?

1994-2021

1994-2021

2020

Question 261

First female to win at the World Championships?

Question 262

Which Scotsman won his first World Championship Title??

Question 263

Which two players "The Barber" and "The Riot" hit the highest finish of 167 in the Players Championship finals?

Question 264

Welshman won the World Grand Prix?

Question 265

Which Belgian won the first tournament behind closed doors, following the Covid-19 restrictions, The World Matchplay?

Question 266

"Duzza" won the Premier League behind closed doors?

Question 267

Which two players "Smiffy" and "Snakebite" hit 9 dart finishes in the Premier League?

Question 268

"Rockstar" hit the highest checkout 164 in the World Grand Prix?

Question 269

And which Portuguese player won the World Grand Prix?

Question 270

Which player was World Youth champion?

2021

Question 271

Who was 2021 World champion?

Question 272

UK Open winner??

Question 273

Premier League from Wales?

Question 274

Former PDC player and former BDO World Chmpion died aged 59 this year?

Question 275

"The Machine" hit a 9 darter in the World Championships?

Question 276

And where was the UK Open held for the first time?

Question 277

Who was World Masters champion?

Question 278

Which Portuguese player was Premier League runner-up?

Question 279

Which two players hit Premier League 9 darters?

Question 280

And which PDC Chairman retired this year?

1994-2021

1994-2021

Answers
1994

1. Dennis Priestley
2. Phil Taylor
3. Circus Tavern, Purfleet
4. Larry Butler
5. Winter Gardens, Blackpool
6. £16,000
7. Kevin Painter
8. BSkyB TV
9. SKOL
10. Russ Bray

1995

11. Phil Taylor
12. Rod Harrington
13. John Lowe
14. World Pairs
15. Jocky Wilson
16. Cliff Lazarenko
17. Proton Cars
18. Cliff Lazarenko
19. John Lowe
20. Phil Taylor

1996

21. Peter Evison
22. Vernons Pools
23. Websters
24. Jamie Harvey
25. Bob Anderson
26. Phil Taylor & Bob Anderson
27. Kevin Spiolek
28. Gary Mawson
29. Dennis Priestley
30. Alan Warriner

1997

31. The PDC
32. Eric Bristow
33. Richie Gardner
34. Phil Taylor
35. Alan Warriner
36. Red Band
37. Raymond van Barneveld & Roland Scholten
38. Rod Harrington
39. Peter Evison
40. Dennis Priestley

1998

41. Rod Harrington
42. Wayne Mardle
43. Phil Taylor
44. Rochester, Ireland
45. Dennis Priestley
46. Rod Harrington
47. Ronnie Baxter
48. Chris Mason
49. SKOL
50. Keith Deller

1999

51. Rod Harrington
52. Peter Manley
53. Ronnie Baxter
54. Paul Lim
55. Bob Anderson
56. Phil Taylor
57. Alan Warriner
58. Shayne Burgess
59. Cliff Lazarenko
60. No 3rd place play-off

2000

61. Rossaire, Ireland
62. Phil Taylor
63. Stan James Bookmakers
64. Eric Bristow
65. Steve Raw
66. Dennis Smith
67. Peter Manley
68. Alan Warriner
69. John Part
70. SKOL

2001

71. Alan Warriner
72. Gayl King
73. John Lowe
74. Richie Burnett
75. Dennis Smith
76. Steve Beaton
77. Citywest, Dublin
78. Roland Scholten
79. Alan Warriner
80. Kevin Painter

2002

81. Phil Taylor
82. Alan Warriner
83. Steve Beaton
84. Colin Lloyd
85. Kevin Painter
86. John Lowe
87. Andy Jenkins
88. Dave Askew
89. Phil Taylor
90. Peter Manley

2003

91. John Part
92. Wayne Mardle
93. Peter Manley
94. Phil Taylor
95. Shayne Burgess
96. Reebok Stadium, Bolton.
97. SKYBET
98. Dave Smith
99. £50,000
100. Roland Scholten

2004

101. Sudden death
102. Wayne Mardle
103. Kevin Painter
104. Roland Scholten
105. Ladbrokes
106. Ronnie Baxter & Peter Manley
107. Mark Dudbridge
108. Alan Warriner
109. Colin Lloyd
110. John Part

2005

111. Mark Walsh
112. Premier League
113. Kevin Painter
114. Mark Dudbridge
115. John Lowe
116. Colin Lloyd
117. Phil Taylor
118. Adrian Lewis
119. Colin Lloyd
120. John Lowe & Eric Bristow

2006

121. Raymond van Barneveld
122. Phil Taylor
123. Roland Scholten
124. Raymond van Barneveld
125. Freddie Williams
126. Barrie Bates
127. Wayne Jones
128. Peter Manley
129. Alan Tabern
130. John Part

2007

131. James Wade
132. Circus Tavern
133. Andy Hamilton
134. James Wade
135. Terry Jenkins
136. Mitchell Clegg
137. Vincent van der Voort
138. Raymond van Barneveld
139. Terry & Andy Jenkins
140. Raymond van Barneveld

2008

141. Kirk Shepherd
142. Alexandra Palace
143. Colin Lloyd
144. John Part
145. James Wade
146. Wayne Mardle
147. Mervyn King
148. Peter Manley
149. James Wade
150. Sid Waddell & Dave Lanning

2009

151. Colin Osbourne
152. Jelle Klassen
153. Steve Beaton
154. Phil Taylor
155. Mervyn King
156. Andy Hamilton
157. James Wade
158. Dennis Priestley
159. Colin Osbourne
160. Robert Thornton

2010

161. Mervyn King
162. Mark Webster
163. Stacy Bromberg
164. Adrian Lewis
165. Raymond van Barneveld
166. Dick Allix & Tommy Cox
167. James Wade
168. Raymond van Barneveld & Co Stompe
169. Simon Whitlock
170. Phil Taylor

2011

171. Phil Taylor
172. Adrian Lewis
173. Gary Anderson
174. Mark Hylton
175. James Wade
176. Aaron Monk
177. Mark Webster
178. Terry Jenkins
179. Richie Burnett
180. Wes Newton

2012

181. Jamie Caven
182. Andy Hamilton
183. Kim Huybrechts
184. Michael van Gerwen
185. Ian White
186. Mervyn King
187. Dave Chisnall
188. Gary Anderson
189. Simon Whitlock
190. Robert Thornton

2013

191. Jamie Caven
192. Dubai
193. Justin Pipe
194. BetVictor
195. Dean Winstanley
196. Adrian Lewis
197. Michael van Gerwen
198. Bruce Spendley
199. Phil Taylor
200. Robert Thornton

2014

201. Terry Jenkins & Kyle Anderson
202. Michael van Gerwen
203. 1st time no Englishman
204. Adrian Lewis
205. Aden Kirk
206. Butlins, Minehead
207. Phil Taylor
208. Stephen Bunting
209. Kim Huybrechts
210. Keegan Brown

2015

211. Gary Anderson
212. Robert Thornton
213. Phil Taylor
214. Michael van Gerwen
215. Simon Whitlock
216. Adrian Lewis
217. Dave Chisnall
218. Martin Adams
219. Max Hopp
220. James Wade

2016

221. Gary Anderson
222. Phil Taylor
223. Mensur Suljovic
224. Rob Cross
225. Alan Norris
226. Robbie Green
227. Jeff Smith
228. Corey Cadby
229. Gerwyn Price, Mark Webster
230. James Wade

2017

231. Michael van Gerwen
232. Peter Wright
233. Dimitri van der Bergh
234. Jonny Clayton
235. Michael smith
236. Michael van Gerwen & Raymond van Barneveld
237. Phil Taylor
238. Mensur Suljovic
239. Gerwyn Price
240. Daryl Gurney

2018

241. Dimitri van der Bergh
242. Rob Cross
243. Gerwyn Price
244. Daryl Gurney
245. Steve Lennon & William O'Connor
246. The Grand Slam
247. Ian White
248. Max Hopp
249. James Wade
250. Gary Anderson

2019

251. Michael Smith
252. Gerwyn Price
253. Mensur Suljovic
254. Rob Cross
255. Nathan Aspinall
256. Luke Humphries
257. Michael van Gerwen
258. Dave Chisnall
259. Gary Anderson, Peter Wright
260. Steve Lennon, William O'Connor

2020

261. Fallon Sherrock
262. Peter Wright
263. Callan Rydz, Ryan Miekle
264. Gerwyn Price
265. Dimitri van der Bergh
266. Glenn Durrant
267. Michael Smith, Peter Wright
268. Joe Cullen
269. Jose De Sousa
270. Bradley Brookes

2021

271. Gerwyn Price
272. James Wade
273. Johnny Clayton
274. Andy Fordham
275. James Wade
276. Milton Keynes
277. Johnny Clayton
278. Jose De Sousa
279. Johnny clayton, Jose De Sousa
280. Barry Hearn

1994-2021

ABOUT THE AUTHOR

Born in Belper, Derbyshire in 1968

Andrew is a keen darts fan,
having seen darts on TV and then becoming
an official on the PDC Pro Tour

I wrote this book at Straws Bridge "Swan Lake", Ilkeston.

Printed in Great Britain
by Amazon